It
sh
bo
te
t
T

IRISH BREAD

Baking for Today

VALERIE O'CONNOR

THE O'BRIEN PRESS
DUBLIN

VALERIE O'CONNOR is a cook, food writer and photographer; she has worked in professional kitchens from Brussels to Malaysia. She is a qualified organic horticulturalist and tutors in food growing, cooking and baking. She is widely published in the press and has appeared as a guest critic on *Masterchef Ireland*. She is the author of *Bread on the Table*, also published by The O'Brien Press.

CONTENTS

Dedication

For Leon and Saoirse, my sons and best critics

First published 2015 by
The O'Brien Press Ltd,
12 Terenure Road East, Rathgar,
Dublin 6, Ireland.
Tel: +353 1 4923333; Fax: +353 1 4922777
E-mail: books@obrien.ie.
Website: www.obrien.ie

Text & Photography © Valerie O'Connor, 2015
Food Stylist: Valerie O'Connor, 2015
Internal author photograph: Sean Curtin
Additional author photographs: Billy Hayes

Copyright for typesetting, layout, editing, design
© The O'Brien Press Ltd

ISBN: 978-1-84717-722-3

8 7 6 5 4 3 2 1
20 19 18 17 16 15

Printed and and bound in Poland by Białostockie Zakłady Graficzne S.A.
The paper in this book is produced using pulp from managed forests

INTRODUCTION

Bread – one of the most universal foods in the world – has deep roots in Ireland. In the days before yeast and bread soda the woman of the farmhouse would grind some wheat and leave it to soak overnight in buttermilk by the hearth before baking it in the bastible pot over the fire in the morning. The advent of bread soda made bread baking a faster process and Irish-style soda breads are some of the quickest and easiest breads for any novice baker to master. Potatoes were always cheaper than flour, so delicious boxty plays an important part in our bread history. The French, famous for their breads, heavily influenced our baking traditions and baguettes were enjoyed in Ireland as far back as the seventeenth century, while another French-influenced bread, the famous Waterford blaa, quickly became part of our repertoire too.

Today bread of all kinds, from yeast breads, rolls and potato breads to traditional brown bread and currant bread have a central place in the kitchens of Ireland.

Try these recipes, and you'll soon be eating warming, nutritious Irish breads and enjoying every crumb!

Bread Lingo:

Essential Kit:

A WEIGHING SCALES: bread baking is quite an exact science, weighing things means better results, a digital one is best. Soda breads are less sensitive to exact measurements.

MEASURING SPOONS: useful for measuring salt, yeast and so on.

TINS: try to find a nice, deep loaf tin to make a nice, deep loaf (alternatively, you can bake loaves in rounds or shape them on a baking tray).

DOUGH SCRAPER: a small piece of plastic, invaluable for mixing, cutting, portioning, cleaning.

LARGE PLASTIC BOWL: for mixing, resting your dough and so on.

TEA TOWELS: it's good to keep a stash of these specifically for bread baking, to use for covering a dough proving in a bowl.

Flour types:

STRONG WHITE FLOUR: flour with a higher protein content, making it more suitable for yeast breads.

PLAIN WHITE FLOUR: better suited to cakes, scones and soda bread.

STONEGROUND WHOLEMEAL: mostly unadulterated, nutty brown; for soda breads.

RYE: dark and distinctly tangy, lower-gluten and works well mixed with wheat.

SPELT: a lower-gluten grain, said to be easier on the digestion of sensitive tummies.

BUCKWHEAT: gluten-free, good for pancakes and batters.

Bread lingo:

SPONGING THE YEAST: activating yeast in warm water until it froths.

KNEADING: working the dough to develop the gluten structure.

RESTING THE DOUGH: the time after the bread is kneaded when it doubles in size.

KNOCKING BACK: a gentle re-working of the dough, folding it and gently kneading it after resting.

PROVING: the final rise of the dough when it's in its shape or tin before baking.

A Note on Yeast

Yeast occurs naturally in the air around us; yeast particles are everywhere. Once science figured out how to grow and multiply yeast it became possible to make it in large volumes and package and sell it. In the recipes that follow for yeast bread, I have given the measurements in grams, as that is how yeast is packaged and sold commercially.

There are three main types of yeast that you can bake with at home, it's an open debate as to the results from one or the other. There are no rules, just use what suits you, or try them all in your own time.

FRESH YEAST: preferred by most real bread bakers this sweetly-pungent stuff comes in a block from good food shops or a kind baker might give you a slice. Keep it in the fridge and use it up quickly.

FAST-ACTION YEAST: comes in sachets measured for one loaf each. It's handy, readily available and works just fine.

BAKER'S YEAST: also powdered, has a slightly stronger flavour and is easy to use.

Fresh yeast is usually added to bread by crumbling it in, while fast-action yeast can be sprinkled in. Depending on the recipe, yeast is often 'sponged' (added to water and allowed to froth up) before being added to the bread mix; baker's yeast is always sponged.

Soda Breads

White Soda Cake

The women of Thomondgate in Limerick were known to be great bakers and would leave their cakes of warm bread to cool on the windowsills of their kitchens; the more cakes you had cooling, the better off you were. Since then, people from the area are known as 'Sodacakes'. Traditionally, the bread was baked over the fire in a cast-iron pot, but you can bake it in any standard oven. It takes literally minutes to throw together and the secret is simple: go easy, don't handle it too much. Use your hand like a claw to bring the few ingredients together and then you're done. The oven needs to be good and hot, as for all bread baking, so make sure you turn it on about half an hour before the bread is ready to go in.

MAKES ONE CAKE/LOAF

INGREDIENTS:

5g/1 generous tsp bread soda
5g/1 tsp salt
600g/1lb 5oz plain flour or white spelt flour

400ml/14floz buttermilk, use real buttermilk leftover from butter-making if you can get it
Preheat the oven to 200C/390F/Gas 6

1. In a large bowl mix the bread soda with the flour and salt.
2. Pour in the buttermilk and, using a claw-like action, bring the flour and buttermilk together until everything is combined and forms a wet ball.
3. Turn out onto a floured surface and, using a little more flour, gently shape the dough into a round, then flatten slightly with your hands. The raising agents will already be at work so if you press your thumb into the dough it should leave an impression.
4. Flour a large baking tray and carefully transfer the dough onto it (place your hand under the dough as you lift it to support it). With a large bread knife, cut a cross into the bread 'to let the fairies out' or let the dough expand.
5. Bake the bread in the preheated oven for 40-50 minutes until golden and hollow-sounding when the bottom is tapped.
6. Cool the bread by an airy window, or under a damp tea towel until it's just the right temperature to cut into thick slices and drown with butter. It's unlikely any will be left to go cold.

Spotted Dog

Not to be confused with Spotted Dick, a steamed, raisiny pudding from England, this is the poshed-up version of soda bread that mothers would bake on a Sunday or on a special occasion; they'd add egg and sugar to a soda bread mixture, turning it into a sweet cake. It's also known as 'Railway Cake' in some parts of Ireland. For an interesting variation you can soak the raisins overnight in some whiskey – Irish of course!

INGREDIENTS:
500g/1lb 2oz plain white flour
1 tsp bread soda
1 tsp salt
300ml/½ pint buttermilk
100g/4oz raisins (if soaking in whiskey overnight, drain before using)
50g/2oz caster sugar
1 large egg
Preheat oven 200°C/390F/Gas 6

1. In a large bowl, sift the flour with the bread soda and the salt, add the sugar and raisins. Next pour in most of the buttermilk, holding a little back in case the dough is too sticky, and crack in the egg.
2. Using your hand like a claw, bring the mixture together until it forms a soft dough, tip it out onto a lightly floured surface. Form the dough into a round, pressing it together as you go and press it down to about 5cm/1 ½ inches in height.
3. Place the dough on a lightly floured baking tray and slice a deep cross into it with a long knife, this will help it to bake through, you can, if you wish poke each quarter with a fork as folklore would dictate.
4. Bake in the pre-heated oven for 40-50 minutes until golden; when it sounds hollow when tapped on the bottom, it's done. To get a softer crust, cool the bread under a clean tea towel that you dampen slightly by flinging a few handfulls of water at it.

Spelt Soda Bread with Dilisk

Spelt has gained popularity in recent years, but it's actually one of the oldest grains on the planet. It doesn't take kindly to being handled too much, so soda bread suits it well. You can make it as you would any soda bread, but make sure that it's fully cooked as your bread will be more moist than the regular white. The best thing about spelt soda is that it keeps for a few days and makes great toast, the crust gets especially crispy in the toaster so slice it, toast it and drown it in butter.

Thanks to places like the Irish Seaweed Centre and people like Prannie Rhatigan, who is an expert in the health benefits and culinary uses of seaweed, we are seeing more seaweed on restaurant menus. This recipe uses much-loved dilisk, which is widely available from street vendors in Limerick and elsewhere in summer. You can also buy it dried and packaged in many good food shops or just harvest your own.

INGREDIENTS:

500g/1lb 2oz white spelt flour

1 tsp salt

1 tsp bread soda

350ml/12floz buttermilk

10g dried dilisk, rehydrated in water for 10 minutes with the water squeezed out and the seaweed finely chopped

Preheat the oven to 200C/390F/Gas 6

1. Combine the dry ingredients in a large bowl and add the buttermilk, stir with your hand to make a rough dough. Next add the dilisk, mixing with your hand to combine. Turn the dough out onto a lightly-floured surface and knead for a minute and shape into a round, pressing it down to about 4cm/1½ inches in height.

2. Place the dough onto a floured baking tray and cut a deep cross into it. Bake for ten minutes at 200°C and then reduce the heat to 180C/350F/Gas 4 and bake for a further 30-40 minutes until the loaf is golden and the bottom sounds hollow when tapped. Leave to cool then slice and enjoy with a topping of smoked salmon, with a squeeze of lemon juice and a sprinkling of black pepper.

3. This loaf keeps surprisingly well, for up to a week. Maybe it's the seaweed that does the trick, but it makes it all the more appealing.

Wholemeal Soda Bread

Wholemeal soda bread is as classic an Irish food as you can get. It's easy to make, fast to get into the oven and requires no bread-baking skill to get right. While it is best eaten warm, it also makes a great base for smoked salmon or cheddar cheese – a snack that's fit for any occasion. The results you get depend on the type of flour that you use – a good-quality stoneground wholemeal will give you a lovely nutty texture and flavour. This recipe mixes half and half wholemeal and white, as a fully wholemeal loaf can be a bit heavy. Feel free to throw in a handful of porridge oats or wheatgerm.

INGREDIENTS:

250g/9oz stoneground wholemeal flour, Ballybrado do an excellent one
250g/9oz plain white flour
1½ tsp bread soda
1 tsp salt
350ml-400ml/12-14floz buttermilk
Preheat the oven to 200C/390F/Gas 6

1. In a large bowl mix the flours with the bread soda and salt.
2. Pour in most of the buttermilk and mix with your hand in a claw-like shape to bring the ingredients together into a sticky ball. Don't handle it too much – some of the dough will stick to your hands, but just rub them together and it will come off.
3. Sprinkle some flour on the table and tip the dough out onto it. Knead it gently for a minute to bring it together into a ball and flatten the ball with your hand until it is about 6cm/2 inches deep

4. Place the dough onto a floured baking tray and cut a cross shape into it using a bread knife.
5. Bake in a preheated oven at 200C/400F/Gas 6 for the first 10 minutes, then reduce the temperature to 180C and bake for a further 30-40 minutes until the loaf is golden brown and sounds hollow when you tap it on its bottom.
6. Cool on a wire rack, traditionally the loaf was cooled standing on its side (pre wire rack days) and draped with a slightly dampened tea towel which resulted in a softer crust.

Easy Oat Bread

If you love the nutty taste of oats and the simplicity of a bread that you don't have to knead then this recipe is for you. It harks back to old flavours and is great with a hunk of cheddar cheese and a mug of tea. It's like porridge on the go – try it with sliced bananas and a drizzle of honey for breakfast, or take it work or school. If you don't eat wheat this is a great bread for you and it keeps for almost a week too. I've shared the recipe with quite a few people and everybody loves it.

MAKES ONE 2LB LOAF
INGREDIENTS:
175g/6oz oatmeal
175g/6oz pinhead oatmeal
120g/4oz oat bran
1½ tsp bread soda/baking soda
1 tsp salt
600ml/1 pint buttermilk
25g/1oz butter, melted
Oven 180C/350F/Gas 4

1. Combine all the ingredients in a large bowl and mix well. Leave the mixture to soak for 30 minutes while you preheat the oven.
2. Grease or oil your loaf tin well and tip the bread mixture into it, sprinkle on a few more oats for a nice finish and bake in the oven for 1½ hours; the longer baking time is due to the wetness of the bread 'batter'.
3. Leave the bread to cool fully before cutting; this is a soft and crumbly bread, but so tasty.

Treacle Bread

Treacle, or molasses is a dark, sticky syrup that comes from sugar cane or sugar beet. It imparts a musky depth and flavour to this bread, which can also be enriched by the addition of a handfull of raisins. Unrefined, organic blackstrap molasses is a superfood, said to improve your hair quality and colour, as well as your 'regularity'. It's also full of iron, calcium, potassium and magnesium, which means it's great for our skin, our bones and our nerves too. All this in a loaf! Time to get baking.

MAKES ONE 2LB LOAF
INGREDIENTS:
250g/9oz white flour/white spelt flour
250g/9oz stoneground wholemeal flour
1 tsp salt
350ml-400ml/12-14floz buttermilk
2 tbsp treacle or mollases
1 tsp bread soda
1/2 tsp ground ginger, optional
Preheat the oven to 200C/390F/Gas 6

1. Put the flours, salt and bread soda in a large bowl and mix well.
In a small pot warm 50ml /2 floz (the amount isn't crucial here) of the buttermilk, add the treacle or molasses and allow it to dissolve.
2. Pour the warmed buttermilk mixture and the remaining buttermilk into the flours and mix well with your hand or a large spoon until the mixture comes together.
3. Depending on the shape of loaf you prefer, you can either scoop the mixture into a buttered and lined loaf tin or tip it out onto a lightly floured work surface, shape it into a traditional round and place on a baking tray.
4. Bake in the hot oven for 10 minutes and then turn the heat down to 180C/F/Gas 5 and bake for a further 30-40 minutes depending on your oven. The bottom of the loaf should sound hollow when tapped.
This bread is a great sweet or savoury snack as it's delicious with all manner of toppings.

Beer Bread

Ridiculously simple and insanely delicious, this recipe was given to me by Niamh Concannon, from Inis Mór on the Aran Islands. I adapted the recipe to include rye flour as it works so well with the sweetness and the beer. Pouring butter all over the bread may seem indulgent, but it makes for the crunchiest crust, full of little nuggets of crispiness and makes the loaf smell just like caramel. Too good to be true? Try it and find out!

MAKES 1 LOAF

INGREDIENTS:

200g/7oz white flour/white spelt

200g/7oz rye flour

25g/1oz sugar

2 tsp baking powder

1 tsp salt

350ml/12floz beer, any type

50g/2oz butter, melted

Prepare a 1.5lb loaf tin by rubbing the inside with butter or oil

Preheat oven 180C/370F/Gas 5

1. In a large bowl mix the flours with the salt, baking powder and sugar, then make a well in the centre and pour in the beer. Mix well with a wooden spoon.

2. Scoop the dough, which should be sticky, into the prepared tin and smooth out the surface slightly.

3. Pour the melted butter over the loaf; it will sneak into any nooks and crannies as well as seeping down around the sides and the bottom of the loaf as it bakes.

4. Bake for 50 minutes to 1 hour. Turn off the oven, pop the loaf out of the tin and return it to the still-warm oven and allow it too crisp up.

5. More butter on thick slices only makes this bread even better!

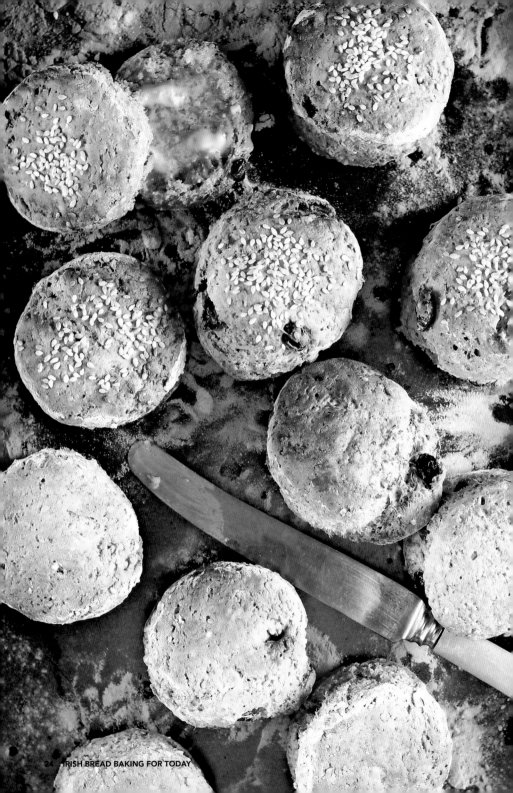

Seeded Soda Scones

Lots of people enjoy varied flours, seeds and flavours in their breads so I've added a few more textures and tastes to this version – add and subtract things as you fancy. These feel healthy so you can feel good about yourself, until you drown them in butter, cream and jam, of course! They have a slight Christmassy feel from the spices.

MAKES 12-14 SCONES
INGREDIENTS:
300g/10oz plain white flour (or white spelt flour)
150g/5oz stoneground wholemeal flour
50g/2oz wheatgerm
100g/4oz mixed dried berries: raisins, cranberries or anything you like

2 tbsp each sunflower seeds and sesame seeds
½ tsp ground cinnamon
1 tsp bread soda
1 tsp salt
300ml/½ pint buttermilk
Milk for a milk wash
Preheat oven to 220C/425F/Gas 7

1. In a large bowl combine all the dry ingredients mixing them thoroughly with your hand.

2. Pour in the buttermilk, using your hand in a claw-like shape to bring all the ingredients together into a slightly sticky dough (depending on the flours you use, you may need to add more, or use less, buttermilk so hold a little back).

3. Tip the dough out onto a lightly floured surface and gently push it outwards until it is about 2cm/1 inch thick, or use a rolling pin, moving it about as you roll so it doesn't stick.

4. I always use a cup to cut out scones as it's so handy. Dip a cup or a cutter into flour and press into the dough, shaking it a bit to release the scone onto a floured baking tray.

5. Loosely gather the remaining dough and re-roll and cut again to use it up.

6. Brush the tops with milk and scatter over a few more seeds or leave plain.

7. Bake in a preheated oven for 10 mins at 220C/425F/Gas 7 and reduce the heat to 200C/400F/Gas 6 and bake for a further 10 mins. The high temperature helps to get a good rise on the scones.

Enjoy these while they're still warm.

Brown Bread Nan Phádaí

Brown soda bread is an institution in Ireland, one that inspires heated discussion amongst (mostly) women about quantities and techniques; some folk like to add wheatgerm and oats, some throw in an egg or a glug of oil. I loved this bread from the first time I tasted it at the wonderful Tígh Nan Phádaí café on Inis Mór, the largest of the Aran Islands, where I was met by six of the eight Concannon sisters, all of whom had their own take on bread recipes. Their mother, who catered daily for her brood of twelve, baked three loaves of this every morning, along with another two cakes of white soda bread. If you think you don't have time to bake, think about Mrs Concannon! This bread is simply perfect, and another easy one. If you visit Inis Mór be sure to stop at the café and try this bread with one of their amazing salads.

MAKES ONE LARGE 2LB LOAF
INGREDIENTS:
700g/1lb 8oz wholemeal flour
1 tsp salt
2 tsp bread soda
100g/4oz wheatgerm

700ml/1 pint 6floz buttermilk
50ml/2floz sunflower oil
Preheat the oven to 190C/375F/Gas 5
Prepare a 2lb loaf tin by rubbing the insides with butter or oil

1. In a large bowl combine the flour with the salt, bread soda and wheatgerm, pour in the buttermilk and oil and mix with a spoon to a sloppy consistency.
2. Spoon the mixture into your prepared tin and bake in the oven for 55-60 minutes.
3. Leave the loaf to cool in the tin for 10 minutes, then remove from the tin and return it to the oven for a further 10 minutes. Allow to cool on a wire rack.
4. This loaf has a delicious, crumbly texture so take care when cutting it. It works with just about everything from smoked salmon to ham or cheese or just plain with butter.

Griddle Cakes

These are also known as 'soda farls', depending on what part of the country you hail from, but the result remains the same. These 'instant breads' will answer any arguments you might have about not having time to bake bread, as you don't even have to bake them. You can make these on a standard frying pan with a good, heavy bottom on it. These are what I make in the morning when we've run out of bread and there's nothing for breakfast. Make these and within ten minutes you have warm, fresh, crusty bread, perfect for breakfast or for making your lunchtime sandwiches.

MAKES 8 GRIDDLE CAKES
INGREDIENTS:
1 quantity of soda cake mix, p 10

1.Put your frying pan on the hob and heat to a medium to high heat. If your pan is too small to cook all the breads at once, simply do them in batches, or use 2 pans.

2.Tip your soda cake mix out onto a floured surface, sprinkle over some flour and knead the mixture for less than a minute, then shape it into a round. Move it round and use a little more flour as you go, pressing the round into a flat of about 25cm/10 inches. Cut it into wedge shapes with a knife.

3.Place the wedges onto the dry frying pan – there's no need to use oil or butter. Leave them to cook for 5-7 minutes and then check their colour underneath. They should be a nice, patchy golden to brown – a bit black is also okay. Using a knife, turn them over and cook for the same time on the other side. They will have puffed up nicely. I cook them on their sides too just to ensure they are well done.

4.Remove from the pan and slice open, enjoy with real butter, with cheese or jam, a big Irish breakfast, or all of the above!

Griddle cakes make the best rasher sandwiches: pack in a couple of slices of bacon and turn it into a BLT with some crispy lettuce leaves and slices of tomato.

Soda Bread Pizza

A revelation! This is the easiest thing since soda bread and gives you a perfect pizza in no time with little effort. You will need a rolling pin and a pizza tray. A batch of soda bread dough makes two medium-sized pizzas, if you only want one, then halve it. This combination of toppings is a take on the classic Italian Spinach and Gorgonzola. Of course you can use any toppings you like – go nuts.

INGREDIENTS:

One batch of soda bread dough (page 10)
Tomato purée, or passata (this works best as it's easier to spread and not too runny)
100g/4oz Cashel Blue cheese, or similar
200g/7oz spinach washed and cooked (or defrosted frozen spinach), with the water squeezed out, then roughly chopped
Preheat the oven to 220C/425F/Gas 7

1. Cut the dough into two equal-sized pieces and roll each one into a ball.
2. Scatter some flour onto the table and roll out the dough into a circle to fit your pizza tray, moving it around bit by bit and flouring it lightly as you go, so that it doesn't stick to the table. The base will puff up in the oven so roll to a thickness of less than 1cm/½ inch.
3. Move the dough onto the tray, do the same with the second piece.
4. Bake the bases in the preheated oven for 5 minutes and take them out, this will stop them from getting soggy.
5. Spread some of the tomato purée or passata around and all over the base using the back of a spoon. Break up the spinach and cheese and scatter these over the base.
6. Bake in a preheated oven for 10-15 minutes until the cheese is golden and bubbling, remove from the oven and slice carefully.
7. You'll probably never order a take-away pizza again, so enjoy the savings as well as the satisfaction. Of course you can top these bases with your own favourite combinations, and you can freeze them too, perfect for emergency lazy dinners.

Soda Bread 'Foccacia-ish'

This is a bread that was suggested to me by several seasoned bread bakers who pointed out that by making a simple soda-bread mixture and adding oil and various flavourings, you could create a delicious, crumbly, seductively simple and impressive bread. So the 'foccacia-ish' was born. I use the much-loved (but not very Irish) sundried tomato, as it goes so well with rosemary, and a goats' cheese from Gabriel Flaherty's delicious Aran Islands Goats' Cheese. You can use any combination of flavours that appeal to you – cheddar cheese and sage, cheese and caramelised onions – enjoy the simplicity and impressed sighs of your friends.

MAKES ONE FLAT LOAF ABOUT 30X20CM (12X8 INCHES)

INGREDIENTS:

500g/18oz plain white flour/white spelt flour

300ml/10floz buttermilk

1tsp bread soda

1 tsp salt

100g/4oz goats' cheese

100g/4oz sundried tomatoes in oil, drained and roughly chopped

50ml/2floz olive oil or rapeseed oil

3-4 springs of fresh rosemary

Sea salt, to finish

Oven 200C/390F/Gas 6

1. Make up the soda bread to a loose dough up to step 2, page 10.
2. Crumble in the cheese and add the tomatoes and oil and mix with your hand to combine. It should be slightly sticky.
3. Flatten the mixture out onto a baking tray, covered with baking parchment, and press it out gently with your fingers until you have a rough shape about 2.5cm/1inch thick.
4. Make some little dents in the dough with your fingers and pour over some extra oil to fill the holes. Drizzle it over the dough,

sprinkle with sea salt and press the rosemary springs into the dough.
5. Bake the bread in a pre-heated oven for 25-30 minutes until it is golden brown all over and looks deliciously inviting with lots of little crumbly edges just waiting to be nibbled off.
6. This bread loves wine!

Note: if you are using dried sundried tomatoes be sure to rehydrate them in some just-boiled water for 30 minutes before draining, chopping and adding to the dough.

Carrot & Dilisk Loaf

Happily, seaweed is making its way back into Irish diets. With the huge number of edible seaweeds available for harvesting on the west coast of Ireland, not to avail of this magnificent free gift of nature would be madness. This recipe comes via Jim Morrissey who wrote *A Guide to Commercially Important Seaweeds on the Irish Coast*. It's a simple 'mix everything up in a bowl' bread and is devastatingly yummy.

INGREDIENTS:

25g/1oz dried dilisk, soaked in water for 10 minutes and all the water squeezed out (keep back some of the 'soak water' for later)
100g/4oz butter, melted
4 eggs
1 large carrot, grated
Pinch sea salt
250g/9oz plain white or spelt flour
1½tsp baking powder
Preheat oven to 190C/375F/Gas 5
Prepare a 1½lb loaf tin

1. Finely chop the dilisk (the easiest way to do this is with a mezza luna).
2. In a large bowl, combine everything and stir well to ensure there are no lumps in the flour. Add a little soak water from the dilisk if it seems too dry – it should look like cake batter.
3. Pour into a greased loaf tin and bake for 50-55 mins, cool on a wire rack and enjoy your taste of the sea.

Boxty

'Boxty on the griddle, boxty on the pan, if you don't eat your boxty, you'll never get a man' - Irish proverb

Irish people from Sligo, Leitrim, Donegal and parts of Tipperary can be heard talking about boxty with much love and many a misty eye. Boxty is made as a loaf in the oven, as pancakes, dumplings and as a griddle bread. The loaf recipe here is easy and supplies you with boxty for a few days.

MAKES ONE LOAF

INGREDIENTS:

1kg/ 2lb 2oz (roughly) peeled potatoes, roosters or pinks are good

300ml/10floz buttermilk

½ tsp bread soda

1 tbsp milk

150g/6oz plain flour (substitute this with white spelt or a gluten-free flour mix)

1 tsp/5g salt

A pinch of sugar

Preheat oven to 180C/350F/Gas 4

Prepare one 2lb loaf tin by buttering the insides well

You will need a clean tea towel, cloth or linen bag to squeeze the liquid from the spuds.

1. Grate the potatoes, then put them into a cloth or linen bag, or even an old, clean pillow case, and squeeze the liquid out vigorously until very little remains.

2. Pop the squeezed, grated spuds into a large bowl, quickly pour over the buttermilk and stir it in; this will stop the potatoes discolouring.

3. Mix the bread soda with the milk and stir this in to the potato mixture, then add the flour, salt and sugar, mixing well with a large spoon to combine.

4. Scoop the mixture into the loaf tin and smooth out the surface with the back of a spoon.

5. Bake in the oven for 60-65 minutes until the loaf is pale golden.

Leave this to cool fully in the tin before turning it out. Slice it the way you would slice cheese, rather than bread, by just pressing down on the knife. Fry the slices gently in butter until they are golden brown and delicious, top with anything from eggs and bacon to a sprinkling of sugar.

7. Variation: Boxty on the Pan (makes approx. 20 small or 4 large pancakes)

To make boxty on the pan, simply fry the boxty batter in melted butter on a heavy frying pan. You can make the pancakes any size from the full frying pan to small, blini-sized ones (pictured here) topped with smoked salmon, crème fraiche and chives, turning this traditional staple into a refined brunch or canapé treat.

Spoon the batter onto the hot pan and cook on a medium heat until bubbles appear on the surface, then flip over and cook the other side.

Oatcakes

Oatcakes came to Donegal in the north of Ireland by way of the Scots. Traditionally, a large round oatcake was dried a short distance from an open fire on a cast iron 'breadiron' or oatcake stand. Oatcakes were known as 'the moon and the stars'; the large oatcake drying in the flame resembled a full moon, full of promise, and the crumbs that remained after the tasty cake was devoured were the stars. Traditionally, an oatcake is baked slowly (at around 140degreesC for about 3 hours, or dried out in an Aga). Here, I'm giving directions on how to bake this delicious, nutritious and easy snack in the simplest way at home, while still remaining traditional. You can store these yummy biscuits for weeks and reheat them in the oven if you want.

MAKES ONE 30CM/12" ROUND, CUT INTO 8 LARGE WEDGES
INGREDIENTS:
250g/9oz medium or fine oatmeal
150ml/5floz boiling water
30g/ 2tbsp butter or bacon fat
A pinch of sea salt
You will need one large pizza tray
Preheated oven 170 degreesC/350F/Gas 4

1. Pour the hot water into a jug and add the bacon fat or butter to melt it.
2. Mix the salt into the oatmeal in a large bowl, then pour in the water and fat. Mix this together first with a wooden spoon and then with your hand to form a firm dough.
3. Lightly scatter some oatmeal over a work surface and gently roll out the dough with a rolling pin into a round, being careful to move it around as you go so that it doesn't stick. When the round is about 30cm/12 inches and 1/2 cm/1/4inches thick, it is ready to bake.
4. Lift the oatcake onto a baking tray, I find a typical pizza tray ideal for this. Cut the round into 8 wedges with a knife or pizza cutter and leave to dry out for an hour before baking. Preheat the oven for half an hour before the oatcake is baked and bake for 45 minutes in the centre of the oven.
5. Oatcakes are a simple and naturally gluten-free snack that can be topped with anything, though they are best with cheddar cheese and a sweet, apple chutney.

Black Pudding & Apple Scones

Black pudding has rightly found its place on many fine dining menus and tastes great with many different accompaniments from apple to scallops. Its crumbly texture works well in a scone, as you can mix it in with the flour and butter crumb; in this scone, the apple gives it a nice sweetness. This tastes great with a tangy cheese and a pint, a meal in itself!

MAKES 12

INGREDIENTS:

400g/14oz plain flour

100g/3oz butter, chilled (I keep some in the freezer for this)

25g/1oz baking powder

150g/5oz black pudding (I love Curragh-chase Black Pudding)

240ml/8floz milk

1 medium-sized eating apple,

1 egg, for egg wash

Preheat the oven to 200C/390F/Gas 6

1. In a large bowl rub the butter into the flour with your fingertips until you have light 'breadcrumbs', add the baking powder and mix lightly with your hand. Break up and crumble in the black pudding, mix it through.

2. Add the milk and mix with your hand or a spatula until you have a light dough. Grate the apple into a bowl and gently squeeze out any excess juice, mix it through quickly to avoid discolouration. The dough may turn an interesting purple colour from the black pudding, but that's ok.

3. Tip the dough out onto a floured surface and knead very lightly until you have a manageable ball, flatten this down slightly, cover and leave to rest in the fridge for 10-15 minutes.

4. Roll out the dough until you have a thickness of about 3cm/1 inch, cut into rounds and lay on a lightly-floured baking tray, brush with beaten egg and bake in the hot oven for 20 minutes until brown and well-risen.

5. These scones have a bit of a 'wow' factor and go great on a brunch table.

Smoked Salmon & Chive Muffins

These savoury muffins are so easy. They take about 5 minutes to get into the oven – perfect for a last-minute snack or as part of a bigger brunch menu. I use white spelt flour, but you can use regular white plain flour for this recipe too. Birgita Curtin from the Burren Smokehouse gave me the idea for these delicious treats.

MAKES 12 MUFFINS
INGREDIENTS:
225g/8oz white flour
5g/1tsp bread soda
½tsp salt
100g/3oz chopped chives
1 egg
75ml/3.5floz melted butter
225ml/8floz buttermilk
125g/4oz smoked salmon, chopped
Preheat the oven to 180C/350F/Gas 4

1. Mix the flour, bread soda, salt and chives in a large bowl.
2. Mix the egg, melted butter and buttermilk in a jug. Pour the wet ingredients into the dry and mix quickly with a fork to combine.
3. Stir in the chopped salmon and mix lightly to distribute well.
4. Divide the mix between 12 well-buttered muffin cases and bake for 20 minutes.
5. Eat these warm as soon as they are baked, not that you'll need much convincing – and keep away from cats as mine ran off with one.

SODA BREADS

Yeast Breads

Basic White Bread

Ordinary yet special, with this dough you can do anything. It provides the backbone for many white bread recipes and it can be shaped in lots of ways, filled and flavoured with just about anything. Get this one right and you'll soon be making rolls, baguettes and pizzas.

MAKES ONE LOAF
INGREDIENTS:
500g/1lb 2oz strong white flour
7g fast-action yeast or 15g fresh yeast
5g/1 tsp salt
350ml/12 floz tepid water
Oven 220C/430F/Gas 7
Prepare a 2lb loaf tin by greasing it well with butter or oil and
grease a large board or table with a little oil for kneading the dough

1. Put the flour into a large bowl, crumble in the fresh yeast and rub it through the flour or sprinkle in the fast-action yeast (pics 1 & 2). Add the salt and pour in almost all of the water (pic 3). Bring everything together with your hand or a dough scraper until you have a craggy mess (pic 4).

2. Turn the mixture out onto an oiled work surface. Knead the dough for 10-12 minutes, resisting the temptation to flour it (pic 5). Get your hands under the mix and lift it up, slap it down and keep doing this until it starts to get smooth. It will seem unruly, but it will start to become elastic as you push and pull: this is the gluten being activated and developing that springy characteristic that yeast breads have. When it begins to become smooth you can lift it up and see if it will stretch easily

(pic 6).

3. If you hold it up to the light and stretch a piece you should be able to see the light and shadows through it; this is called the window-pane effect.

4. Shape it roughly into a ball (pic 7) and pop it back into the mixing bowl, cover it with a tea towel (or piece of cling film rubbed with a little oil) and place in a draught-free place for an hour. This time is called 'resting' the dough (pic 8).

5. After an hour the dough should have doubled in size and will leave an indent if you push into it with your finger. It gets exciting at this stage as you see your efforts paying off. Carefully scoop the dough out with your hand, put it on the table and firmly press it, folding it over itself a few times to push the air out and develop the gluten a bit more (pic 9 & 10). Pop the dough into the prepared tin and return it to its warm spot for another hour, again covered with a tea towel. This is the time that the dough 'proves' (pic 11).

6. Half an hour before baking time preheat the oven – it needs to be good and hot for bread. If you have a water sprayer have it handy as a spray or splash of water in the oven creates steam and gives a lovely crust to your loaf.

Your dough should be pushing up the tea towel, eager to get into the oven to be baked. Carry it, like a precious prize, to the warm kitchen.

7. With a very sharp knife, swiftly slash a few lines into the top of your loaf. Pop the tin into the centre of the preheated oven, spray a few jets of water (or pour an egg-cup of water into the bottom tray of the oven). Bake the loaf for 40-50 minutes, depending on the temperament of your oven, until it is a nice, brown colour.

8. Take the loaf from the oven; it should tip out easily from its tin so that you can tap its bottom. If it sounds hollow, it's cooked. Put it back into the oven without the tin for a further five minutes to crisp up the crust all round. Cool it on a wire rack, or on top of the tin, until you can't wait any longer and just have to slice it. Have your butter at the ready and devour happily, little else will bring you so much pride in the kitchen.

PIC 1   PIC 2   PIC 3   PIC 4

PIC 5   PIC 6   PIC 7   PIC 8

PIC 9   PIC 10   PIC 11   PIC 12

Irish Breakfast Pizza

It's the full Irish, in your hand! The perfect morning-after breakfast where a fry-up meets fast food, but with the cheekiness of a take-away. Who doesn't secretly love pizza for breakfast? When the pizza is ready the egg yolk is still runny so it runs around and mingles with everything when you cut or bite into it. You can go as basic or as flash on the ingredients as you want, from shop-bought own-brand bacon and sausages to ethically-reared, free-range pork.

MAKES TWO 14-INCH PIZZAS OR FOUR 7-INCH INDIVIDUAL PIZZAS
INGREDIENTS:

One batch of rested white yeast dough, page 49

Flour for rolling out the dough

50g/2oz tomato purée,

3-4 medium-sized fresh tomatoes, thickly sliced

6 cooked sausages, sliced about ½ inch thick

6 rashers streaky bacon, uncooked, cut into pieces

4oz/100g mushrooms, sliced

Eggs, 4 for the large pizza, 1 each for the small ones

Fresh parsley and olive oil to finish

Preheat the oven 220°C/450°F/Gas 7

1. Flour a work surface, tip the dough onto it, knock it back, then cut into 2 or 4 equal pieces; roll the pieces into balls and leave to prove again for 30 minutes.

2. Flatten the balls, then roll out the bases by teasing them out with your fingers, moving the dough around and sprinkling lightly with flour so that they don't stick, until you have the sizes that you want. Lay them on pizza or baking trays.

3. Spoon on the tomato purée and spread it with the back of a spoon. Lay on the tomato slices.

Scatter on the rest of your toppings, except the eggs. Bake in the hot oven for 10 minutes.

4. Take the pizzas out of the oven, crack the eggs onto them, then return them to the oven for five minutes. Get them out of the oven, drizzle over a little olive oil and a sprinkle of fresh parsley and devour. May require a beer, or at least a mug of tea!

Sage & Onion Plait

Yeast doughs lend themselves to all sorts of shapes and flavours. Sage and onion is a classic combination often used in bread stuffing for a roast chicken, but it works really well in this lovely light and airy loaf that's also a feast for the eyes. The deep, earthy flavours make this a perfect loaf for a wintery day and it toasts really well too.

MAKES ONE LOAF
INGREDIENTS
One batch of white yeast dough rested, as per page 49
1 medium-sized white onion, finely chopped
25g/1oz butter, for frying
5g/a small handful of fresh sage leaves, finely chopped
Milk or egg for brushing
Oven 200C/390F/Gas 6

1. In a frying pan melt the butter and cook the chopped onion slowly over a medium heat until it is soft and sweet. Sprinkle in the sage and stir. Remove the pan from the heat and allow the mixture to cool.

2. Knock back the rested dough and work the cooled sage and onion mixture into it by kneading gently. Leave the dough to rest for a further 10 minutes.

3. Divide the dough into three equal pieces, place them on a floured surface and roll each piece into a ball, then into a long length of about 30cm or longer, as it will spring back.

4. To make the plait, line up the dough 'sausages' side by side, with space in between and pinch the ends of the 3 sausages together.

5. Now bring the right length over the middle one, followed by the left length over to the right and continue on swiftly until you have a plait.

6. Lay the loaf on a floured baking tray and cover lightly with a floured cloth, return it to a draught-free place to rise for a further 50-60 minutes while you preheat the oven.

7. Using a pastry brush, brush the loaf all over with milk or a lightly beaten egg.

8. Bake the loaf at 200C/400F/gas 6 for 10 minutes and turn the heat down to 180C/350F/Gas 4 and bake for a further 30-40 minutes until the loaf has a nice golden sheen and sounds hollow when tapped underneath.

Blaas & Tayto Blaa

'Blaas' are lovely floury baps, native to Waterford and parts of Kilkenny. The blaa is a legacy from the Huguenots who settled in the area in the 17th century. They traded heavily in wheat and developed the blaa, derived from the French word for white – *'blanc'* – as a means of using up leftover pieces of dough. The blaa is the only Irish bread under the PGI (Protected Geographic Integrity) seal, which means that only those produced within this region, using the age-old techniques, can be called blaas. These puffy, white rolls are usually bought in large batches, still clinging together in swathes.

The lovely blaa bakers, Dermot and Micheál Walsh, shared this recipe with me after a visit to their M&Ds bakery in Waterford city. Having spent three years as a student in Waterford sustained by these rolls it's a joy to be able to reproduce them at home.

MAKES 24 BLAAS

INGREDIENTS:

55g fresh yeast/3 x 7g sachets fast action yeast

570ml/1 pint water

1kg/2lb 2oz strong white bread flour

25g salt/5tsp salt

Oven 230C/450F/Gas 8

1. Sponge the yeast in 100ml tepid water to activate it, then top up to 570ml/1 pint with cold water; the ideal temperature is straight from the tap.

2. Make the dough by adding all the flour and the salt and bringing everything together into a craggy mess. Tip this out onto a floured work surface and knead well for 10-12 minutes. This is a stiffer dough so will really work your muscles! Leave the dough in a bowl, covered with a cloth, to rise for 2 hours.

3. Tip the dough out onto a floured table and knock it back to get most of the air bubbles out.

4. Cut the dough into equal pieces (you can do this by cutting it in 2 and then repeating the process until the dough has made 24 pieces, or you can use a digital weighing scales to portion off 65g/3oz pieces).

5. Roll each one of these into a little ball and leave them to prove again (preferably sitting in some flour), sprinkle with flour and leave covered for another 40-60 minutes.

6. This is a fun bit – take each ball and flatten it with the palm of your hand, it will deflate and you will hear it 'fart' a little. Place these flat pieces edge to edge, barely touching, on floured baking trays, sprinkle with flour again, cover and leave to prove one last time while the oven heats up.

7. Pop the trays into the hot oven, turn the heat down to 200C/400F/Gas 6 and bake for 20-25 minutes until they just barely change colour; they will remain mostly white due to the flour.

Variation: Tayto Blaa

Tayto is the most-loved crisp brand in Ireland and the Tayto blaa is a recognised regional speciality in Waterford. All you need is a blaa and half a bag of Tayto crisps per person, plus butter, if you like.

1. Slice the blaa open horizontally. If you fancy some butter then butter it on both sides.

2. Pile as many Tayto as you can onto the bottom half of the blaa then swiftly and deftly (you don't want fallout) pop on the top half of the blaa. To make eating this easier, squish the blaa down with your hand and hear all the Taytos crunch together. Enjoy a real 'Irish food' experience.

Note: if you can't get your hands on blaas, then Tayto sandwiches on any white bread work equally well.

Potato Bread

Putting potatoes in bread works so well; it's something Irish people have always done, from potato cakes and farls to this beauty here – a classic white loaf. This loaf is much lighter than you'd expect and has a lovely springy texture. The toast is the best ever and the potatoes seem to keep it fresh for longer, not that it ever lasts long! There are often a few spuds left over from dinner and if you get into the habit of keeping the water – which adds to the starchiness and springiness of the bread – you'll have no excuse not to throw on a loaf of this. Try and get your hands on a nice, deep 2lb loaf tin, and you'll have a decent-sized, 'normal-looking' slice, perfect for sandwiches and to convert those who like packet 'bread'.

MAKES ONE LARGE LOAF
INGREDIENTS:

225g/8oz cold, boiled potatoes

600g/1lb 5oz strong white flour, or you can use a mix of white and wholemeal if you want a brown loaf

1x7g sachet fast-action yeast/15g fresh yeast

10g/2 tsp salt

225ml/8floz leftover potato water (or regular water)

Oven 220C/430F/Gas 7

1. In a large bowl, mash the potatoes, then add the flour, crumble or sprinkle in the yeast and the salt. Mix these together and add the water until you have a craggy dough, just like any normal white bread dough.

2. Tip it out onto the table. You may need to add a bit more flour to get a workable dough, so just keep doing that until it starts to come together.

3. Knead the dough for at least 10 minutes until it becomes smooth and elastic, then pop it into a clean, oiled bowl and cover with a tea towel or a piece of oiled cling film and set aside for an hour or until the dough has doubled in size.

4. Tip it back onto the table and knock the air out of it by punching it gently a few times. Prepare the tin by oiling or buttering the inside well and pop your dough into it, covering the tin with a tea towel. Preheat the oven.

5. After 30 minutes the dough should be risen, so put the tin in the centre of the oven and

bake for 10 minutes before turning down the heat to 200C/400F/Gas 6 and baking for a further 30 minutes.

6. Check the loaf is done by tapping it on the bottom – if it sounds hollow, it's ready. Once it's out of its tin, you can put it back in the turned-off oven for a few minutes to ensure an all-over crispy crust.

7. Slice, slather with butter, make toast, make sandwiches and make it again and again!

Potato & Milk Rolls

Don't be fooled by the innocently-plain appearance of these little rolls, they are eye-rollingly delicious, soft and yielding. These rolls were a tea-time indulgence in the big houses of Ireland as they are made with expensive ingredients of milk, butter and eggs, sophisticated yeast and white flour, as well as the common man's potato. Though the recipe may seem complicated, the resulting rolls are worth the effort; the crust is soft and the inside just waiting to be laden with fresh cream and jam. You can make this dough the evening before and keep it in the fridge under a cloth, taking the bowl out in the morning to knock it back and shape your rolls while the oven heats up. Ideally, use up your leftover potatoes to make the dough and if you get into the habit of keeping and freezing the leftover water from boiling potatoes, this way you will always have a great booster for your yeast doughs.

MAKES 12-14 ROLLS

INGREDIENTS:

15g fresh yeast/7g fast action yeast

150ml/5floz reserved cooking liquid from the potatoes, warmed to room temperature

1 tbsp honey

600g/1lb 5oz strong white flour, plus some extra for dusting

1 tsp salt

50g/3oz butter, cold and cut into small pieces

150ml/ 5floz milk, warmed to room temperature

150g/6oz mashed potatoes

1 egg

Oven 200C/Fan 390F/Gas 6

1. Sponge the yeast (allow it to froth up) in the potato water, then add the honey.

2. Mix the flour with the salt and rub in the butter with your fingertips until the mixture resembles fine breadcrumbs. Next, pour in the yeasty potato water and the milk and add the mashed potatoes. Mix this together well with your hands and turn the dough out onto a floured surface kneading it and adding small amounts of flour as you go until you have a workable dough, then knead for 10-12 minutes and flour the finished dough.

3. Pop the dough into a lightly oiled bowl and cover with a cloth. Leave it to rise for at least an hour in a draught-free place, or overnight in the fridge.

4. Turn on the oven, carefully tip out the dough onto a lightly floured surface and divide it into 12 equal pieces. Flatten the pieces with the palm of your hand to make a round roll and gently roll each one out like a fat sausage.

5. Lay the rolls on two baking trays, leaving plenty of space for them to rise, cover them with clean tea towels dusted with flour and leave to rise again for 30 minutes.

6. Bake the rolls in the hot oven for 15-20 minutes until golden brown and enjoy them while still warm and soft.

Guinness, Treacle & Walnut Bread

A chef friend, Paul Cosgrove, gave me this recipe; I'd tried many times to get a recipe that highlighted the characteristics of our favourite pint, and this is a great one. Guinness works best in a yeast bread, making the most of the malted flavours and the brewer's yeast that make up this wonderful stout. The treacle brings out the typical burnt-barley taste of the brew and the walnuts give a lovely sweet little crunch. This bread tastes great with a big slab of mature cheddar and a pint of Guinness, naturally!

MAKES ONE LARGE LOAF

INGREDIENTS:

200g/7oz coarse ground wholemeal flour (I like Ballybrado best)
300g/10oz strong white flour
5g/1tsp salt
15g fresh yeast/7g fast-action yeast
2 tbsp treacle
300ml/10floz Guinness – from a can, bottle or draught
50g/2oz walnuts, chopped
Oven 200C/390F/Gas 6

1. Put the flours and salt in a large bowl and either rub in the fresh yeast or sprinkle over the fast-action yeast. Then add the treacle and Guinness and begin to bring all the ingredients together with your hand, or a dough scraper.

2. When you have a craggy dough, tip it out onto an oiled surface and knead it for 10-12 minutes, or do the kneading in a mixer, but finish it by hand so you know the feel of your dough. Sprinkle over the walnuts and keep kneading until they are fully incorporated.

3. Put the dough in a bowl, cover it with clingfilm or a tea towel and allow it to double in size for at least an hour.

4. Knock back the dough by punching it down and folding it over a few times. Shape it into a round and lay it on a floured or oiled baking

tray, covered with a cloth. Leave to rise again for 50-60 minutes, meanwhile preheat the oven for 30 minutes before baking.

5. Slice a few long cuts into the loaf with a bread knife or blade. Bake for 20 minutes and then turn the oven down to 180C/350F/Gas 5 for a further 20-30 minutes, checking to see if the loaf is baked by tapping it on its bottom, if it sounds hollow, it's cooked.

6. This bread has a lovely robustness and is very satisfying to bake.

Easy No-Knead Spelt Bread

I bake this bread constantly at home and in my baking classes – it's so easy when you don't have to do any kneading. This is a great introduction to yeast breads as you get all the benefit of a good rise with none of the effort. This bread freezes really well, so if you'd like to make two loaves and freeze one, simply double everything.

INGREDIENTS:

500ml/18floz tepid water
1 tsp honey
1½ tsp fast-action yeast
500g/18oz wholemeal spelt flour
Approx 50g/2oz porridge oats
1 tsp salt
2 tbsp mixed seeds
Preheat the oven to 200C/390F/Gas 6
Prepare a 2lb loaf tin

1. In a jug measure 200ml/7floz hot water, dissolve the honey, then top up to 500ml/16floz with cold water, add the yeast and leave it to 'sponge' (froth up) for 10 minutes.

2. In a large bowl mix the spelt flour with the oats and salt, pour in the yeasty water and mix well to combine. The mixture will be wet and puffy, a bit like a thick porridge.

3. Spoon the mixture into the prepared tin, sprinkle the mixed seeds over the top, cover with a tea towel and leave aside for 40 mins to 1 hour until it has risen to just below the top of the tin. Any warm, draught-free place is good for this. Have the oven preheating for 30 minutes before the loaf is due to go in.

4. Put the tin into the oven and bake at 200C/400F/Gas 6 for 10 minutes, then turn the temperature down to 180C/350F/Gas 4 and bake for a further 50 mins.

5. When the loaf is baked, remove from the oven and leave to cool in the tin for about 20 minutes. Run a knife around the inside of the tin, tip out the loaf and return it to the cooling oven to crisp up the crust.

Multiseed Flowerpot Loaves

Being a keen gardener with a yard full of terracotta pots, I thought it only right to include these cute flowerpot breads – featuring seeded bread, of course! I bake these breads in gardeners' terracotta pots. The pots must be seasoned for baking first: wash them in hot water, then dry them, oil them well and bake them in the oven at 150C/300F/Gas 2 for 30 minutes and leave them to cool. You can keep these pots for baking these cute loaves any time, and you can use any yeast dough. This recipe makes 3 small loaves in pots with an 8cm/3inch diameter.

INGREDIENTS:

100g/3oz mixed seeds: sunflower, pumpkin, linseed, sesame
300g/11oz mixed grain or malthouse flour
200g/7oz strong white flour
1 tsp/ 5g salt
15g fresh yeast/7g fast-action dried yeast
330ml/10floz tepid water
Oven 200C/400F/Gas 6

1. Soak 60g of the seeds in some water, this helps make them digestible. Keep the rest aside for topping the breads.

2. Mix the flours and salt together in a large bowl, crumble in the fresh yeast or sprinkle over the fast action one. Pour in the tepid water and make your dough as usual by kneading the mixture on an oiled surface for 10 minutes until smooth and pliable.

3. Cover the dough with a cloth or tea towel and leave in the bowl to rise.

4. Oil and line the insides of the pots with baking parchment by cutting out small discs for the bases and long rectangles for the insides.

5. When the dough is risen, knock it back and sprinkle over the soaked seeds, kneading them until they are fully mixed in. Divide the dough into 3 and form 3 balls. Dip the top of each ball into a small bowl of water and then into the bowl of remaining seeds, place each ball – seeds upwards – into the pots, cover them

with a cloth and leave to prove for a further 50 minutes; while they're proving, you can preheat the oven.

6. Bake the pots in the hot oven for 30 minutes; their smaller size means they will bake more quickly.

7. These look great on a dinner party table, especially one outside in summer, and make nice little round slices, perfect for patés. If you have smaller pots then bake them in the same way and give one to each guest.

Sally Lunns

These sweet, puffy little buns are native to Waterford and a legacy from the Huguenots who settled there in the 17th century. According to local bakers, these treats are called 'Sally Lunns' after the sun and the moon (*soleil et lune*) due to their yellow hue (from the use of butter and eggs) and their dark side, provided by the addition of raisins. The bun is also popular in Wales, which also had a heavy presence of Huguenots; in Wales, legend has it that a young girl named Sally Lunn sold these buns on the streets of Bath, but the Waterford bakers claim the first explanation, which one you choose is up to you.

MAKES 12-14 BUNS

INGREDIENTS:

15g fresh yeast/7g fast action dried yeast

200ml/7oz water

50ml/2floz milk

75g/3oz caster sugar

7g salt

500g/1lb 2oz strong white flour

1 egg

50g/2oz butter

100g/4oz raisins

FOR THE SUGAR SYRUP:

100ml/4floz water

100g/4oz sugar

Oven 200C/390F/Gas 6

1. Allow the yeast to 'sponge' (froth up) in the water for about 10 minutes, then warm the milk slightly and add it to the yeasty water along with the sugar, salt, flour, egg and butter and combine everything until you have a rough dough. Knead for about 10 minutes, until the dough is smooth and elastic, then add the raisins and knead again to combine. Cover the dough and leave in a draught-free place for an hour.

2. Turn the dough out onto a lightly floured work surface and fold it over a few times to get some air out of it. Divide the dough in 2 and then divide each piece into 6 and roll them into tight little balls. Cover with a cloth and leave aside to rise for another 30-40 minutes.

3. Once they have risen, press your hand down gently on each ball until it flattens slightly, then lay the rounds side by side in a baking tin big enough to take them all (about 20x30cm/8x12inches), cover and leave to rise again for at least 30 minutes while you heat up the oven.

4. Bake the buns for 15-20 minutes until golden brown. Meanwhile make the sugar syrup by gently heating the sugar and water in a pot until the sugar is dissolved, and simmering for 2 minutes. Brush the buns with the syrup immediately they are out of the oven.

5. Split these open while still warm and spread with butter to enjoy a little bit of history.

If you like the idea of a loaf of this bread, simply knock back your rested dough after step 1, shape it into an oblong and place it in a buttered, 2lb loaf tin. Leave this to rise for 50-60 minutes and bake in the preheated oven for 10 minutes, then turn the heat down to 180C/350F/Gas 4 for a further 50 minutes. This is a moist dough, so it's important to ensure it's well baked. This loaf is delicious sliced and buttered, toasted or in French toast or Irish coffee trifle (page 86).

Nettle Pesto Bread

Nettles are everywhere on this fine island of ours – free and abundant; we all have fond memories of falling into them as children and rubbing ourselves with dock leaves to ease the stings. But we can also do so many delicious things with our wild and wonderful free foods. Nettle soup in May is said to be great for the blood and contains more iron than a steak! Just be sure to go foraging in spring and early summer and cut only the top, young parts of the plants.

NETTLE PESTO BREAD

INGREDIENTS:
1 batch rested white yeast dough (page 49)

NETTLE PESTO
100g/3.5oz prepared nettles (cooked and chopped)

1 clove garlic

1 tsp salt

50g/2oz pinenuts (hold back a few for decoration)

100ml/3½ floz olive or Irish rapeseed oil

50g/2oz grated Parmesan or similar hard cheese

Salt & freshly-ground black pepper, optional

Oven 200C/390F/Gas 6

1. Handle nettles with care, using thick rubber gloves at all times until they are cooked. Wash the nettles and pop them into a pot of boiling water for 3-5 minutes to cook, by now the sting is gone so you can use your bare hands. Rinse them in a colander and squeeze out as much excess water as you can, then chop them finely.

2. In a food processor, or with a mortar and pestle, crush the garlic clove with a little salt, add the pinenuts and crush gently, stir in the olive oil and the nettles, add the cheese and stir well, maybe add a little more salt and black pepper.

For the loaf

1. Take your rested dough from its bowl and knock it back, gently easing out any air bubbles to give it a little boost. Spread it out into a rectangle with your fingers.

Spread the pesto over the bread, leaving a gap of about 5cm/2inches from the edges. Next, lift up one side of the dough and roll it into a chubby loaf shape.

2. Pop the loaf into an oiled loaf tin and cover and leave to prove for another 40-60 minutes. Bake in your preheated oven for 50 minutes until it's brown – and probably a bit green!

3. Pestos and flavoured oils can be used in so many ways with breads, as toppings for bruschettas, drizzled onto a pizza or anything that grabs you, it's robust and cheap to make and fun too.

Sweet Things

Sweet Scones

As a baker you're nothing without a scone! It always seems to be one of those things that some people are naturally gifted at; the doorbell rings, an unexpected visitor arrives, the kettle goes on and a batch of freshly-baked scones is whipped up and baked by the time the cups and plates are laid out. This recipe results in lovely, crumbly scones with a soft, sweet inside. This one delivers on all counts.

MAKES 12

INGREDIENTS:

400g/14oz plain flour

100g/4oz butter, chilled (I usually keep some in the freezer for this)

100g/4oz caster sugar

25g/1oz baking powder

180g/6oz sultanas, or mixed fruit

180ml/6floz milk

80ml/3floz cream,

1 egg, for egg wash

Preheat the oven to 220C/425F/Gas 7

(The heat of the oven is crucial to the rise of the scone)

1. In a large bowl, rub the butter into the flour with your fingertips until it resembles light 'breadcrumbs', add the sugar, baking powder and fruit and mix lightly with your hand.

2. Add the milk and cream and mix with your hand or a spatula until you have a light dough.

3. Tip this out onto a floured surface and knead very lightly until you have a manageable ball, then flatten it down slightly, cover and leave to rest in a cool spot for 10-15 minutes.

4. Roll out the dough to a thickness of about 3cm/1½ inches, cut into squares or rounds and lay on a lightly-floured baking tray. Brush the rounds with beaten egg and bake in the hot oven for 10 minutes, then turn the temperature down to 200C/390F/Gas 6 for 10 minutes, or until golden brown and risen.

5. These taste fantastic drowned in butter, or go the extra mile and get some good jam and clotted cream.

Summer Pudding

Summer brings an abundant and delicious harvest of fresh berries, bursting with flavour and goodness. They're so tasty on their own as a snack, but this dish turns them into a real talking point, just by adding some leftover white bread and a little sweetness. Make this the day before you want to eat it so that all the flavours get to mingle really well, and the pudding is set and ready to eat. Frozen berries also work perfectly well so you can make this delicious dessert any time of year.

INGREDIENTS:

750g/1lb 6oz fresh or frozen mixed berries, strawberries, blackberries, raspberries, redcurrants, blackcurrants

150g/5oz caster sugar

8-10 slices semi-stale white bread, crusts cut off

2 tbsp elderflower cordial (optional)

Fresh berries, to decorate

You will need one pudding bowl of 10cm/4inches diameter

1. Put the fruit and sugar in a saucepan and bring to a simmer, cook gently for 3-4 minutes, leave aside. Strain the fruit, keeping the juices.

2. Oil the insides of the pudding bowl and line it with clingfilm, leaving enough overlap to cover the top of the bowl. Cut a circle of bread to fit in the bottom of the bowl, then cut the rest of the bread slices in half. Dip the circle in the fruit juices and lay it in the bottom of the bowl. Continue lining the pudding bowl with the bread slices, laying them along the insides, overlapping them as you go.

3. Spoon the fruit into the centre and pour over any remaining fruit juice, and the cordial (if using).

4. Lay the remaining bread slices on top of the fruit to cover everything, ensuring there are no gaps.

5. Fold over the clingfilm, then get a small plate or saucer to fit on top of the bowl, and weigh it down with a tin of beans or something similar. Leave in the fridge overnight to set, preferably on a larger plate to catch any juices that spill out.

6. Remove the plate from the top of the bowl and peel off the clingfilm. Turn the bowl upside-down onto a large plate or dish and lift off the pudding bowl. Peel off the clingfilm and decorate the pudding with fresh berries and drizzle over any remaining juices. Enjoy this summer delight with fresh cream or vanilla ice cream.

Tea Brack

In Ireland, people traditionally eat Barmbrack at Halloween. 'Barmbrack' is a fruity yeast loaf that at Halloween has lucky and unlucky charms concealed in it. In our house, we waited with bated breath to see who would get them; the stick meant you would have an unhappy marriage, the coin signified imminent wealth, poverty would befall whoever got the rag – but everyone wanted the ring, which meant you would get married within the year, no matter your age or marital status! This version of brack is slightly lazier, as it's not made with yeast, but it's much tastier, and involves soaking the fruits overnight to plump them up and make them extra juicy. Though quite rich, this tea bread is always served sliced and thickly covered with real butter.

INGREDIENTS:

300g/10oz mixed dried fruits: raisins, sultanas, cranberries

300ml/10floz hot black tea

300g/10oz white flour or white spelt

200g/7oz light brown sugar

1 tbsp baking powder

2 tsp mixed spice or cinnamon

1 egg

25g/1oz butter, melted

2 tbsp honey, to glaze

Oven 180C/350F/Gas 4

Prepare a 28cm/10inch springform tin

1. In a large bowl mix the fruits then pour in the hot tea and leave the fruit soaking overnight, or for at least 4-5 hours.

2. When the fruits are fully soaked, preheat the oven. Sieve the flour, baking powder, mixed spice or cinnamon and sugar into a large bowl, crack in the eggs and drizzle in the melted butter.

3. Give everything a good stir to mix it up and turn the mixture into the prepared tin.

4. Bake in the centre of the preheated oven for 1½ hours, checking that the top isn't burning (cover it loosely with tinfoil if it starts to burn).

5. Brush the cake with honey while it's still warm and allow to cool fully before slicing.

6. Wait for witches to call, or have a big slice with a nice cup of tea.

Bread & Butter Pudding

Bread and butter pudding re-emerged in recent years and is a popular choice in fine dining restaurants where chefs love to get experimental with the flavours and serving techniques. Traditionally it's made with a simple custard base and needs little else to create a warming, rich and delicious hot desert. This recipe transforms ordinary, everyday food into an indulgent, moan-inspiring dish.

SERVES 4

INGREDIENTS:

300ml/10floz milk

1 vanilla pod or 1 tsp vanilla extract

3 eggs

50g/2oz caster sugar

100g/4oz butter

50g/2oz raisins

6-8 slices leftover white bread with crusts cut off

Preheat oven 180C/350F/Gas 4

You will need a pudding or pie dish, about 20cm/8inches diameter.

1. In a saucepan, gently heat the milk with the vanilla pod or extract. Don't let it boil.

2. Turn off the heat and leave the pod to infuse for at least 10 minutes, then remove it.

3. Whisk the eggs with the sugar in a bowl and slowly add the infused milk to the mixture.

4. Butter the inside of the pudding dish well.

5. With softened butter, butter both sides of the bread slices and cut them into triangles. Layer the slices, overlapping, in the dish until all the bread is used up. Sprinkle over the raisins.

6. Gently pour the egg and milk mixture over the bread, taking care to cover as much surface as you can.

7. Bake in the oven for 25-30 minutes until it's nice and puffy with crunchy dark bits at the edges.

8. Serve this treat with whipped cream or rich vanilla ice cream.

Irish Coffee Trifle

This recipe occurred to me when I had some leftover Sally Lunn loaf (p 71) to use up, though a sweet dough like brioche or a yeast raisin bread will work just as well here. It's a little bit Tiramisu, with the marscapone to give the trifle just the right richness. The whiskey and coffee make it 100 per cent Irish, and cheeky too. You can make a single trifle in a bowl, but I've chosen to make cute individual trifles in glasses here. These can be made a day ahead and kept in the fridge. This dessert saves you a lot of effort as you have cake, coffee and a drink in one!

MAKES 4-6 INDIVIDUAL TRIFLES OR 1 20 X 20CM TRIFLE

INGREDIENTS

200ml very strong coffee

50g/2oz brown sugar

100ml/4floz Irish whiskey

6-8 slices leftover, slightly stale sweet bread

250ml/10 floz whipping cream

250ml/10 floz marscapone

25g/1oz icing sugar

Cocoa for dusting

1. Dissolve the sugar into the hot coffee, add the whiskey and set aside to cool.

2. Cut circles out of the slices of bread that will fit comfortably inside the width of the glass you're using. You'll need three rounds for each glass.

3. Using an electric mixer, mix the cream with the marscapone and icing sugar until the mixture is thick and creamy.

4. Dip the rounds of bread into the coffee mixture, then place one in the bottom of each glass, adding a little extra liquid to make sure it stays good and moist and to give the diner a nice whiskey treat at the end of their desert.

5. Using a piping bag, pipe a layer of the cream mixture on top of the bread. Repeat the layers until the glasses are full, finishing with a layer of cream mixture and dust lightly with some cocoa powder.

6. If you prefer to make one shallow, tiramisu-style trifle simply lay the slices of bread in the dish and spoon over enough coffee mixture to soak the bread evenly. Cover with a layer of cream mixture and repeat for at least two layers.

Potato Donuts

'Podonuts', 'Doughtatoes' – whatever you call them, these are amazing! Take one bite into the paper-thin shell, crispy and sweet, then into the fluffy, puffy insides – you won't be able to stop at one! Donuts are made from yeast dough, just like any regular bread, but adding mashed potato to any yeasted dough takes it to levels of lightness and fluffiness that you can usually only dream of. This is a great recipe for a rainy day; it takes time, but it's fun, the results are so worth it and you end up with quite a feast.

MAKES 30-34 DONUTS

INGREDIENTS:

200ml/8 floz milk

50g/2oz butter

3 tsp/15g fresh or 1x7g sachet fast action yeast

600g/1lb 5oz strong white flour

5g/1tsp salt

50g/2oz caster sugar, plus extra for dredging

2 medium eggs

225g / 9oz cold mashed potatoes, made without butter, milk or seasoning

Cooking oil, for frying

You will need a deep frying pan or deep fat-fryer (the oil needs to be about 7cm/2½ inches deep)

1. Gently heat the milk in a pan to around body temperature (if you test it with your finger it should feel neither hot nor cold), then turn off the heat, add the butter and allow it to melt.

2. In a large bowl, mix the yeast with the flour, sugar and salt, pour in the milk mix, the eggs and the mash. Knead as normal for 10-12 minutes until your dough is smooth and elastic. If using an electric mixer finish the kneading by hand. The potato will make the dough a little stickier so add a little extra flour if you need to.

3. Leave the dough to rise for 1 hour, until your finger leaves a dent in it when you press it. Knock back the dough on a floured surface by folding it over a few times and punching it a little. Shape into a sausage. Cut the dough in 2 and then in 2 again until you have about 30-34 pieces, or portion them off in 30g pieces. Roll each one into a ball and leave to prove on oiled trays, leaving space in between them so they don't stick together, cover with a cloth that's lightly dusted with flour, for about 30 minutes.

4. Once the dough balls have risen nicely (handle them carefully as they may be delicate) you can heat up the oil for frying. You will know the oil is hot enough if you drop a piece of bread into it and it fizzles immediately.

5. Have a couple of large plates covered in kitchen paper by your side as you begin frying, pop the first batch of donuts in and let them get nice and brown before turning them over, and lifting them out with a slotted spoon to drain while you make the rest.

6. Now sprinkle lots of caster sugar into a large dish and dredge the donuts in it, covering them liberally on all surfaces. You can add some cinnamon to the sugar if you like. These donuts are fillable, if you want to fill them with custard or jam simply fill a piping bag with a small nozzle with your chosen filling, insert the nozzle into the side of the donut and fill carefully.

Stuff your face with these beauties, you didn't go to all this effort for nothing!

Brown Bread Ice Cream

This dessert became quite 'the thing' in fine dining restaurants in the 90s, and it's hard to understand why it disappeared from favour. It's an incredibly easy way to make an impressive and delicious treat and use up leftover brown bread. This works best with brown soda bread – Brown Bread Nan Phadaí (p 26) would be delicious because of its lovely nutty texture. You can go ahead and make your own vanilla ice cream as a base if you wish, but I just use my favourite shop-bought brand and mix it in. Cheating? Yes, but with results as easy and tasty as this who cares?

MAKES 1 LITRE
INGREDIENTS:
1litre/2pint tub good-quality vanilla ice cream
200g/7oz leftover brown bread, made into crumbs
100g/4oz caster sugar
Preheat the oven 180C/350F/Gas 4

1. Line a baking tray with baking parchment.
2. In a bowl, mix the breadcrumbs with the sugar and then spread them on the tray, put this in the oven and leave for 10 minutes, then take out the tray and give the crumbs a good mix around.
3. Repeat this every five minutes until the crumbs taste nice and crunchy, it will take about 30 minutes (they will be brown already so it's harder to tell from the colour), then tip them onto a plate to cool.
4. Allow the ice cream to soften at room temperature for about 15 minutes, then stir it up with a large spoon and sprinkle in most of the cooled crumbs, leaving some aside for extra crunch on top. When it's all fully mixed return the ice cream swiftly to its tub (you don't want it to be completely melted) and return to the freezer to harden. With its crunchy, cake-y chunks you don't need anything else with this, just a spoon.

Acknowledgements

With thanks to the Concannons of Inis Mór, Aran, my favourite place to work; Maggie Hanley for letting me photograph on her farm; Christian Baldenecker for helping with the afternoon tea; Sean Molony for holding the reflector on the dilisk loaf in Quilty, Co. Clare. Thanks also to Nicola Kennedy, a true friend and a great collector, for loaning me some beautiful fine Irish bone china and linen, which tells its own stories of our lesser-known and refined past. Eternal thanks to all the food producers in Ireland who work hard to hone the delicious produce from this beautiful country, from smoked salmon to black pudding, goats' cheese to pickled herrings, all of which go perfectly, with bread! And special thanks to my editor, Helen.

Bibliography

Allen, Darina, *Forgotten Skills of Cooking* (Kyle Cathie Ltd)

Bertinet, Richard, *Dough* (Kyle Cathie Ltd)

David, Elizabeth, *English Bread and Yeast Cookery* (Grub Street)

Ingram, Christine & Shafter, Jenine, *The Complete Book of Bread and Bread Machines* (Hermes House)

Lawson, Nigella, *How to be a Domestic Goddess* (Random House)

Manning, Anneka, *Mastering the Art of Baking* (Murdoch Books)

Ptak, Claire & Dimbleby, Henry, Leon: *Baking and Puddings* (Conran Octopus)

Rhatigan, Prannie, *Irish Seaweed Kitchen* (Booklink)

Ross, Ruth Isabel, *Irish Baking Book* (Gill & Macmillan)

Index